Coaching People

Pocket Mentor Series

The books in this series offer immediate solutions to the challenges managers face every day. Each book is packed with handy tools, checklists, and real-life examples, including a Test Yourself section to help identify strengths and weaknesses. For all readers eager to address the daily demands of work, these books are ideal.

Books in the series:

Leading Teams
Running Meetings
Managing Time
Managing Projects
Coaching People
Giving Feedback
Leading People

Coaching People

Expert Solutions to Everyday Challenges

Harvard Business School Press

Boston, Massachusetts

Library of Congress Cataloging-in-Publication Data

McManus, Patty.
  Coaching people : expert solutions to everyday challenges.
          p. cm. – (Pocket mentor series)
  "Patty McManus, mentor"—P.
  Includes bibliographical references.
  ISBN-13: 978-1-4221-0347-0 (pbk. : alk. paper)
  ISBN-10: 1-4221-0347-1
  1. Employees—Coaching of. 2. Mentoring in business. I. Harvard Business
School Publishing Corporation. II. Title.
  HF5549.5.C53M38 2006
  658.3'124—dc22

                                    2006034446

The paper used in this publication meets the requirements of the American
National Standard for Permanence of Paper for Publications and
Documents in Libraries and Archives Z39.48-1992

Contents

How to Manage a Coaching Session   31

Prepare before the session, define objectives, direct the discussion, and assist in developing an action plan.

How to Customize Your Coaching   39

Know when to use different styles for different situations and people.

Tips and Tools   47

Tools for Coaching People   49

Worksheets to help you plan and manage coaching.

Test Yourself 57

A helpful review of the concepts presented in this guide. Take the test before and after you've read through the guide to see how much you've learned.

Answers to test questions 60

To Learn More 63

Additional titles of articles, books, and CD-ROMs if you want to go more deeply into the topic.

Sources for Coaching People 69

Notes 71

For you to use as ideas come to mind.

Mentor's Message: Coaching as a Lifelong Learning Process

Welcome to *Coaching People: Expert Solutions to Everyday Challenges.* Coaching can take lots of different forms, from a onetime conversation for quick advice to an ongoing exploration that spans weeks or months. However you coach others, I think you'll find the tools and concepts in this guide helpful. You'll be able to make the most of the time you have with those you coach so that you meet their unique needs and feel confident using a process you can rely on.

However, I have to warn you—even though the essentials of coaching are simple, they are hardly easy. Enter here and you begin a path of lifelong learning. It seems I never stop refining my coaching skills. The good news is that you probably already know more than you think you do. In fact, I'll bet you have at least one good coaching role model, and that's half the battle.

Here's a suggestion for how you might begin this learning process. Take a minute to get a picture in your mind of someone who has really helped you achieve your personal or professional aspirations. Think of someone you'd consider an excellent coach who came along at the right time. What did this person do or say when she was coaching you? How did you know she was on your side? How did she get inside your head to find out what you were thinking? If she was ever tough about giving you feedback, what made it OK? If she gave you good advice, what made it effective? If you can answer any of these questions about the actions of a good coach—and incorporate them into your coaching style—you're well on your way to making a big difference in others' lives.

In my years as a leadership consultant, I have noticed a pattern in all my client systems that bears telling. From first-time supervisor to senior-level executive, leaders have an enormous and direct impact in their one-on-one communications with staff. In fact, one's supervisor has the potential to strengthen an employee's relationship to the job and the organization. If I feel that my boss is looking out for me, has my interests and goals in mind, and can help me optimize my potential, chances are I bring more loyalty and spirit to my work.

I hope you find this book enlightening and fun.

Patty McManus, Mentor

Patty McManus has provided leadership and organization development consulting to organizations for nearly twenty years. She has focused on developing collaborative change processes and skill in for-profit, public, and nonprofit sectors. Ms. McManus served as an internal organizational development consultant at University of California, Berkeley; Kaiser Permanente; and Apple Computer. She joined Interaction Associates in 1997 as a senior consultant. She provides numerous organizations with leadership training and coaching, collaborative and learning process design, and change consulting. She has an MS in Industrial/Organizational Psychology from San Francisco State University. She feels lucky that one of her favorite and most entertaining topics is her work.

Coaching:
The Basics

What
Is Coaching?

You cannot teach a man anything.
You can only help him discover it within himself.
—Galileo Galilei

What do we mean by the word *coaching* in the world of management? The manager who acts as coach is helping the *coachee* to reach a goal, but there are some special elements of coaching in the business world that a football coach or singing coach might not use.

What coaching is and what coaching is *not*

As a manager you are called on to work with people in many different capacities, and your role as a coach is one such function. Coaching is an opportunity to contribute to another person's development. It is a two-way partnership where you both share knowledge and experience in order to maximize the coachee's potential and help her achieve her goals .

Because coaching is based on mutual agreement, it is not appropriate for every situation. More direct managerial intervention is required when

- a new or inexperienced employee requires explicit direction on a task

Coaching is…
- a means for learning and development.
- guiding someone toward her or his goals.
- the mutual sharing of experiences and opinions to create agreed-upon outcomes.

Coaching is not…
- an opportunity to correct someone's behaviors or actions.
- directing someone to take actions to meet goals.
- being the expert or supervisor with all the answers.

Source: Adapted from Interaction Associates, Inc.

- a staff member has clearly violated company policy or organizational values

- there is no improvement in performance after multiple coaching sessions

Good coaching avoids manipulation and coercion. Coaching asks what is right *as well as what works.*

—Stan Hustad, performance coach and leader PTM Group

Coaching with Purpose

You coach or ask for coaching when you believe that working together will lead to improved performance. Through coaching, you can help others to

- maximize individual strengths (for example, build on analytical skills)

- overcome personal obstacles (for example, address fear of public speaking)

- reach their full potential through continuous learning (for example, learn how to use the Internet for business research)

- achieve new skills and competencies to become more effective (for example, develop more advanced communication skills)

- prepare themselves for new responsibilities (for example, acquire leadership skills)

- manage themselves (for example, find ways to improve use of time)

- clarify and work toward performance goals (for example, learn to set more realistic goals)

- increase their job satisfaction and motivation

The benefits of coaching can go beyond the individual coachee and support your team and the organization itself by:

- improving working relationships between manager and direct reports

- developing more productive teams

- using organizational resources more effectively

When should coaching take place?

Unlike goal-setting and performance reviews, which are formally scheduled quarterly or yearly, coaching is ongoing and occurs as the need or opportunity arises. Sometimes, you schedule coaching sessions about particular situations. More often, you coach informally as you interact with direct reports and peers in person, by phone, or through e-mail.

Tip: Take advantage of every opportunity—provide coaching when people ask for it.

How to Know
When to Coach

At times, a manager has to focus more on people than on tasks, and this is one of those occasions. When you sense or see or hear that a direct report is

- having problems accomplishing his job
- becoming a bit bored with the routine
- causing friction among your team
- stumbling while working on certain tasks

start thinking about how you can help. The first step is to understand the situation, the person, and the person's skills. Then you can act together to improve the situation, the person's self-image, and his skills.

Observing

Observing a coachee will enhance your ability to offer informed, relevant, timely advice. You need to observe the person's behavior both informally (for example, during a meeting) and formally (for example, on joint sales calls). You are trying to identify strengths and weaknesses in two ways:

1. how the coachee's behavior affects his coworkers
2. how the coachee's behavior affects his own ability to achieve his own goals

As you observe, you will be forming theories about what is happening, but don't make judgments or assumptions too quickly. Try to be a neutral observer.

Test your theories through further observation. Where appropriate, discuss the situation with others to get their perspectives. Finally, be sure to check your theories and share your data with the coachee.

The observation process

1. Prepare preliminary questions. When you observe an individual's behavior, think about answers to the following questions:

   - What is the person doing or not doing effectively? Be as precise as you can.

   - What effect does the person's behavior have on achieving your group's goals or individual objectives?

   - What effect does the behavior have on other members of the team?

2. Avoid premature judgments. You are trying to be a neutral observer, so think in terms of actual events and not about causes.

Tip: Coaching is ongoing. Don't expect to solve a problem in a single coaching session.

What Would YOU Do?

Sales Slump

WHEN CARL WALKED INTO HIS OFFICE, there was Rita sitting hunched in a chair, a glum look on her face. "I think I'm losing it, Carl. I'm just not closing as many sales anymore." Rita was a knowledgeable rep and a good one, but Carl suspected that he knew what the problem was. Carl suggested she talk less during her sales calls, listen to the customers more, and avoid overwhelming them with too much detailed product information. Then he advised her to cheer up—everyone goes through their slumps—he knew Rita would get back into the swing of things soon.

Carl prided himself on his coaching, giving nuggets of advice and boosting morale. So he was a little disheartened a couple of weeks later when Rita returned, even more depressed, with the same problem. She'd done what he had suggested but she was still getting the same lousy results. Obviously a pat on the back wasn't going to be enough. Carl knew he needed to take a different approach, but what more could he do to help Rita improve her performance?

EXAMPLE: For example, on the one hand, a *judgmental* manager might conclude after observing a team meeting that a direct report "is domineering, doesn't respect others in the group, and blocks valuable contributions from others."

On the other hand, an *observant* manager might see that the direct report "interrupts others frequently during meetings, and coworkers are quiet and make few contributions." In the second case, the manager is making observations about people's behavior and not creating unverified conclusions.

3. Reflect on your observations. After careful observation, you may decide that the person *does* have a problem that coaching could resolve. Or you could conclude that the problem lies not with the original team member, but with another person or even with team dynamics.

4. Test your theories. Continue to observe, particularly if you don't feel comfortable with your perceptions. Where appropriate, discuss the situation with others—trusted peers or colleagues—to get their perspectives. Consider any cross-cultural issues that might help you better understand the situation or person involved.

5. Examine your own motives. Before suggesting coaching to someone you think is a problem performer, take a close look

at your own behavior first. Ask yourself how you might be contributing to the problem.

- **Unrealistic expectations.** Ask yourself, *"Am I using my own performance as a yardstick to measure others?"* You've probably progressed in your career by setting high expectations and achieving an outstanding track record. Assuming that others have identical motivations or identical strengths may be unrealistic and unfair.

- **Interfering feelings.** Ask yourself, *"Is it hard for me to identify with someone who's having a problem?"* Be self-aware and recognize when your own feelings, such as anger or frustration, may keep you from appreciating what someone else might be feeling—and may cloud your observational and analytical skills.

- **Failing to listen.** Ask yourself, *"Have I passed up chances to listen?"* People don't always know what kind of help they need or exactly how to ask for it. When you see an opportunity, take the time to listen actively to direct reports.

- **Failing to praise.** Ask yourself, *"Have I remembered to give positive feedback?"* Often managers forget to take the time to look for opportunities to give positive feedback. Over time, an absence of positive feedback could contribute to a direct report's problem behavior or attitude.

- **Acting on your words.** Ask yourself, *"Am I a good role model?"* For example, if you view good listening skills as important in cultivating good teamwork, then model those skills for others every chance you get.

6. Conduct a reality check. A reality check with a trusted peer can be helpful. As you become more aware of your own development needs, you'll become a better manager and coach.

7. Discuss your observations with the coachee. Be careful to describe observed behavior when discussing a problem, rather than the coachee's attitude or character. For example, begin by saying, *"This is what I observed."* Remember to address the impact of behavior on group goals and on other people. For example, you might suggest that *"If I were in that team member's shoes, I might think…."* When describing behavior and its effect on other people, be truthful and straightforward, yet calm and supportive.

Tip: Act as a good role model.

Your direct reports may be mimicking your behavior.

A Coach's Self-Evaluation Checklist

The questions below relate to the skills and qualities needed to be an effective coach.
Use this tool to evaluate your own effectiveness as a coach.

Question	Yes	No
1. Do you show interest in career development, not just short-term performance?	✓	
2. Do you provide both support and autonomy?	✓	
3. Do you set high yet attainable goals?	✓	
4. Do you serve as a role model?		✓
5. Do you communicate business strategies and expected behaviors as a basis for establishing objectives?		✓
6. Do you work with the individual you are coaching to generate alternative approaches or solutions that you can consider together?	✓	
7. Before giving feedback, do you observe carefully, and without bias, the individual you are coaching?		✓
8. Do you separate observations from judgments or assumptions?		✓
9. Do you test your theories about a person's behavior before acting on them?		✓
10. Are you careful to avoid using your own performance as a yardstick to measure others?		✓
11. Do you focus your attention and avoid distractions when someone is talking to you?	✓	
12. Do you paraphrase or use some other method to clarify what is being said in a discussion?	✓	
13. Do you use relaxed body language and verbal cues to encourage a speaker during conversations?	✓	

Question	Yes	No
14. Do you use open-ended questions to promote sharing of ideas and information?	✓	
15. Do you give specific feedback?	✓	
16. Do you give timely feedback?	✓	
17. Do you give feedback that focuses on behavior and its consequences (rather than on vague judgments)?		✓
18. Do you give positive as well as negative feedback?		✓
19. Do you try to reach agreement on desired goals and outcomes rather than simply dictate them?		✓
20. Do you try to prepare for coaching discussions in advance?	✓	
21. Do you always follow up on a coaching discussion to make sure progress is proceeding as planned?		✓
TOTALS	11	10

When you have these characteristics and use these strategies, people trust you and turn to you for both professional and personal support. If you answered "yes" to most of these questions, you are probably an effective coach. If you answered "no" to some or many of these questions, you may want to consider how you can further develop your coaching skills.

What You COULD Do.

Remember Carl's dilemma?

Here's what the mentor suggests:

Carl may need to do a better job of helping Rita assess why she's not getting the results she wants. Who knows, maybe her clients have changed, and she hasn't changed with them. Maybe she's picked up some unproductive habits that she's unaware of. He can try a few things. He could ask Rita her best guess about what has changed. He could offer to observe her on a sales call. He could offer to walk through her strategy and approach before or after her next client meeting—or some combination of all three. Then he'd be able to provide specific feedback and suggest some small changes she could make. Carl could close the loop by suggesting they check in after her next call to see how it went and determine her next moves.

How to Develop Coaching Skills

Good managers use coaching skills as part of their repertoire. The focus is on cooperation and facilitation of the other person's development. Coaching involves creating a comfortable environment where action plans can be developed together.

To become the most effective coach possible, work on mastering the following skills:

- listening actively

- asking the right questions

- advocating your opinions

- giving feedback as a coach

- receiving feedback as a coach

- building agreement

"I never could figure out why people didn't seem to follow my advice much. When I started to learn about the true art of coaching, it became painfully clear that my brilliance was falling on deaf ears because I hadn't done a bit of inquiry to learn what they were thinking, what they'd already tried, what their biggest priority was. Inquiry has made all the difference. It turns out most people want less advice but more opportunity to explore their own thinking with a caring coach who is paying attention."

—Patty McManus, consultant, Interaction Associates

Tip: Those who coach regularly, coach better. Find opportunities to develop your coaching skills.

Listen actively

As a coach you need to be tuned into the other person's feelings and motivations. You do this through *active listening*. Active listening encourages communication and puts other people at ease. Active listening also clarifies what's been said to avoid misunderstanding. As an active listener, give the coachee your full attention by following these guidelines:

- Maintain eye contact with the coachee.

- Smile to put the other person at ease.

- Avoid anything that will distract your attention. For example, don't answer the telephone. Only take notes if necessary.

- Be sensitive to body language such as posture and arm position. Is the person tense or relaxed?

- Listen first and evaluate later.

- Do not interrupt the other person except to ask questions to clarify and to encourage him to continue.

- Repeat in your own words what you think the other person has said.

- Wait until after he has finished talking to plan your responses.

?What Would YOU Do?

No Sign of Change

A S PAULA SAT THROUGH TONY'S PRESENTATION, bored as a rock, the sad truth slowly dawned on her. He was making the same mistakes now that he had been making six months ago! His nose was buried in his notes. He was droning on and on, and he had not incorporated a single visual into the entire presentation! Yet they had spoken about his need to work on this very skill. Tony had told her that public speaking was something he just couldn't do. Paula had assured him that with hard work and practice he *could* do it. He believed her and he kept trying. So why, then, was he still so bad at it? Was there something more she could do to help him improve?

Tip: Coach your direct reports; don't play psychologist. It's not appropriate and you are probably not qualified.

Ask questions

Asking questions is a valuable tool for understanding the other person and determining his or her perspective. Use both open-ended and close-ended questions. Each yields a different response.

Notice how this manager asks open-ended questions to uncover the employee's perspectives, listens actively to what is said, and then checks for understanding.

Ilka: Gonzalo, how do you feel the project is going?

Gonzalo: Pretty well. We're on schedule.

Ilka nods her head.

Gonzalo: But it's tight. There's no room to spare.

Ilka: Because…?

Gonzalo: Because when Jenna left, no one was hired to replace her.

Ilka: And because you've lost one person…?

Gonzalo: It's going to be really hard to meet the deadline.

Ilka: Are you saying that you'll deliver on time, but it will be difficult? Or that you may not be able to meet the deadline?

Gonzalo: Well, I think we can make the deadline, but there is a chance we might miss it.

Ilka: And if we want to be sure to finish on time…?

Gonzalo: We'd need more help.

Ilka: Perhaps we could look into getting some temporary help.

Tip: Ask a lot of open questions.

Most managers ask too few.

Ask open-ended questions. Open-ended questions invite participation and idea sharing. Use them to

- explore alternatives: *"What would happen if…"*

- uncover attitudes or needs: *"How do you feel about our progress to date?"*

- establish priorities and allow elaboration: *"What do you think the major issues are with this project?"*

When you want to find out more about the other person's motivations and feelings, think of open-ended questions. Through this type of questioning you can uncover your coachee's true concerns. This, in turn, will help you formulate better advice and ideas about how you can help her.

Use close-ended questions carefully. Close-ended questions lead to "yes" or "no" answers. Use them to

- focus the response: *"Is the project on schedule?"*

- confirm what the other person has said: *"So, the critical issue is cost?"*

Advocate for your opinions

Effective coaches offer their ideas and advice in such a way that the person receiving it can hear them, respond to them, and consider their value. It is important to advocate for your opinions in a clear and balanced way.

---

advocate *v* **1:** to argue a position **2:** to plead in favor of

---

- Describe the individual's situation as you see it.

- State your opinion about the situation.

- Make the thoughts behind your opinion explicit, and share your experiences.

- Encourage the other person to provide her perspective.

Your collaboration with the coachee will be most successful if you use both inquiry and advocacy in your communications. Over-reliance on inquiry can result in the participants' withholding important information and positions. Conversely, if you emphasize advocacy too heavily, you create a controlling atmosphere that can undermine the coaching partnership.

Give feedback as a coach

Feedback differs from advocacy in that you are responding to a specific behavior or action rather than presenting and arguing your position on the overall problem or need for change. Giving and receiving feedback is a critical part of managing in general, but it is an especially important part of coaching. This give-and-take goes on throughout the coaching process as you identify issues to work on, develop action plans together, and assess the follow-through.

When giving feedback—whether positive or negative—try to do the following:

- Focus on behavior—not character, attitudes, or personality. Describe the other person's behavior and its effect on projects and/or coworkers. Avoid judgmental language, which only makes people defensive. For example, instead of saying, *"You're rude and domineering,"* say, *"I observed that you interrupted Fred several times during each of our last three meetings."*

- Be specific. Avoid generalizations. Instead of saying, *"You did a really good job,"* you could say, *"The transparencies you used for your presentation were effective in getting the message across."*

- Be sincere. Give feedback with the clear intent of helping the person improve.

- Be realistic. Focus on factors that the other person can control.

- Give feedback early and often in the coaching process. Frequent feedback that is delivered soon after the fact is more effective than infrequent feedback.

"Good coaches have coaches of their own. I can remember one time when I received timely and exquisite coaching. My boss gave me feedback about a self-defeating communication habit I'd gotten into. Because she was compassionate, caring, and clear as a bell in her de-

scription, I was able to see exactly what she was talking about and ex-plore why I was caught in this pattern. I was then able to shift my style and get the kind of results I intended."

—Patty McManus, consultant

Receive feedback as a coach

You also need to be open to feedback on how effective you are as a coach. Coaches who are able to request and process feedback about themselves learn more about the effectiveness of their management styles and create greater trust among members of their groups. To improve your ability to receive feedback:

- Ask for specific information. For example, *"What did I say that made you think I wasn't interested in your proposal?"* or *"How were my suggestions helpful to you?"*

- When you ask for clarification, do so in a way that doesn't put the other person on the defensive. Instead of saying, *"What do you mean I seemed hostile to your idea?"* say, *"Could you give me an example?"*

- Be willing to receive both negative and positive feedback.

- Encourage the other person to avoid emotion-laden terms. For example, *"You said that I am often inflexible. Give me an example of things I do that give you the sense that I am not flexible."*

- Don't be defensive. Only justify your actions if asked. Tell the other person when you've gotten all the feedback you can ef-fectively process.

- Thank the person for being willing to share feedback with you, both positive and negative. This will improve trust and model productive behavior to the person you are coaching.

Build agreement

Agreements are the foundation of coaching. You build agreements in the beginning as you commit to working together, and throughout your relationship as you pursue the coaching objectives. The agreement process includes all the above activities from initially recognizing the need for coaching to observing to listening actively to one another and collaboratively coming to agreement about the issues and resolutions.

There has to be agreement between the coach and the coachee for the coaching process to work. However, agreement can range from skeptical acceptance to wholehearted involvement. When your coachee sees progress being made on changing behavior or building skills, then agreement will become easier to achieve.

Active Listening Self-Assessment

Are You an Active Listener?

Coaches who listen actively tend to get the most out of their coaching discussions and tend to be better coaches overall. Use this self-assessment to think about how actively you listen. Check the box next to the number in the column that best describes your listening habits.

While someone is talking, I:	Usually	Sometimes	Rarely
Plan how I'm going to respond.	❏ 1	☑ 3	❏ 5
Keep eye contact with the speaker.	☑ 5	❏ 3	❏ 1
Take notes as appropriate.	❏ 5	☑ 3	❏ 1
Notice the feeling behind the words.	☑ 5	❏ 3	❏ 1
Find myself thinking about other things while the person is talking.	❏ 1	❏ 3	☑ 5
Face the person who is talking.	☑ 5	❏ 3	❏ 1
Watch for significant body language (expressions, gestures).	☑ 5	❏ 3	❏ 1
Interrupt the speaker to make a point.	❏ 1	☑ 3	❏ 5
Am distracted by other demands on my time.	❏ 1	☑ 3	❏ 5
Listen to the message without immediately judging or evaluating it.	☑ 5	❏ 3	❏ 1
Ask questions to get more information and encourage the speaker to continue.	❏ 5	☑ 3	❏ 1
Repeat in my own words what I've just heard to ensure understanding.	☑ 5	❏ 3	❏ 1
Totals for each column:	30 +	15 +	5
Grand Total =	50		

Scoring:

44–60 = You are an active listener.

28–43 = You are a good listener with room for improvement.

12–27 = You need to focus on improving your listening skills.

Source: AT&T School of Business. *The Supervisor: Coaching for Success.* AT&T School of Business, 1995.

What You COULD Do.

Remember Paula's dilemma?

The mentor suggests:

Yes, this is a tough one! Paula has invested time in Tony, but she's not seeing a positive return. He's not even doing the basic things they agreed on months ago. First, she may need to manage her own emotions so that she doesn't come off as frustrated or hopeless. Then, after asking if he's willing to hear some feedback, Paula could give him two or three clear examples of his actions during his talk and their impact on her (she probably wouldn't say she was "as bored as a rock"). She could then use inquiry to learn about his experience while preparing and speaking, and what he's willing to try changing. Given his terrible fear of public speaking, he may need to take much smaller steps to improve, like practicing his opening lines out loud or even doing a run-through with her the next time he's getting ready to give a presentation.

How to Manage a Coaching Session

Much of the coaching you'll do will be informal and impromptu as situations arise. However, as part of the process, both coach and coachee arrange for some formal sessions to plan and review the coaching process.

Prepare for the coaching session

Arrange for a private room or space where both of you will feel comfortable. Make sure there will be no interruptions during your meeting; for example, remove or disable telephones and mobile phones.

Both participants need to create a discussion plan for the session. As you prepare your plan, consider the following:

- In what area is the coaching needed?

- What are the desired outcomes?

- What is at stake?

- What is the particular purpose of this session? Initial planning? Establishing an action plan? Reviewing progress?

- What are potential difficulties, and how will you handle them?

If you are the coach, ask the coachee if she suggests that you do any further preparation prior to the session, and offer her your own suggestions about how she might prepare.

Tip: Set ground rules up front. For example, agree that what you say is confidential.

Conducting the coaching session

It was hard to let go of the notion that, as a coach, I was supposed to be all-knowing and full of perfect answers. For a while, I needed some one-liners to state my intention about this while I was still getting used to the idea. Examples for me were, "I have some ideas but I'd like to hear from you first" or "How about if I act as a sounding board for a while to let you think out loud?" It turned out that these are also simple contracting statements so we both know how to play our parts.

—Patty McManus, consultant

Coaching is a partnership. During the coaching session, as you and the other person work on improving job performance or achieving new skills, remember those attainable goals. Now is the time to use those coaching skills you've been practicing!

- Make sure you have a shared understanding of the session's goals.

- Keep the tone positive. Emphasize your sincerity in wanting to help the other person.

- Exchange perspectives on the situation or opportunity at hand. Present relevant data you have gathered during your observation of the coachee.

- Listen actively to his thoughts and explanations.

- Share your advice and suggestions.

- Give the individual an opportunity to present his ideas and respond to yours.

- Discuss the pros and cons and agree on desired outcomes.

- Gain the individual's commitment to create an action plan, and set a follow-up date to review the plan.

Tip: If you initiated the coaching, identify the areas of need. If the other person initiated the coaching, ask for details about the desired area for development.

Develop an action plan

The person being coached develops the action plan. Your role in supporting the plan can include

- helping to ensure that the goals are realistic

- helping the coachee prioritize the tasks needed to achieve the goals

- highlighting potential obstacles and brainstorming potential solutions

- determining what additional coaching support will be required

The Coach's Planning Form

Use this form before a coaching session. Take the time to specify exactly what you hope to achieve and how you intend to go about it.

Discussion with: Sonia Patel　　　　　　　**Date:** March 1

Areas Where Coaching Is Needed *(base this on observations)*:

Efficient planning of daily crew schedules.

Purpose of Coaching Session:

Review steps in planning.

Desired Outcomes:

Prepare for next coaching session on overcoming bottlenecks in scheduling.

Why It's Important to Coach *(e.g., What is at stake? What are the consequences?)*:

Production line needs to improve efficiency and quality.

Potential Difficulties	Methods for Handling
1. Sonia may want to move too fast and cover too much too quickly.	1. Set an agenda for the coaching session.
2. Sonia may not want to hear that her way is not the best way.	2. Give Sonia autonomy in learning the process.
3. Sonia may feel anxious about missing work.	3. Get supervisor's OK for her to be away from her post.

Specific Actions

1. Make the agenda specific and stick to it.

2. Have Sonia first work out the scheduling steps herself, and then guide her in the missing or misplaced spots.

3. Let her know at the start of the session that her supervisor has cleared time for this session.

Adapted with permission from AT&T.

Action-Planning Worksheet

Use this worksheet to establish an action plan that is agreeable to both you and the person you are coaching. It is critical to include specific measures of success and a target review date for any actions to be completed. Examples are included.

Action to Be Taken	Measure(s) of Success	Review
Employee will refrain from interrupting colleagues during staff meetings.	• No interruptions observed during two successive meetings. • No complaints from other staff members.	12/15
Employee will take more time to explore client's needs before matching potential products to those needs.	• Number of questions asked to identify needs. • Need clarified prior to offering potential solution.	After two more joint client meetings

Work together on areas of agreements. This is your opportunity to demonstrate your listening skills as you support the other person in creating and committing to the action plan.

Tip: Set small milestones to build confidence and maintain motivation.

Coach beyond the session

Effective coaching includes follow-up that checks progress and evaluates effects on the coachee and the team. Your follow-up should include

- asking what is going well and what is not
- sharing your observations and reinforcing positive progress
- looking for opportunities for continued coaching and feedback
- identifying possible modifications to the action plan
- asking how the coaching session was helpful and what could be improved

---

Tip: Keep the coaching focused to one or two topics.

Coaching Session Evaluation

Use this tool after the coaching session to evaluate its effectiveness and to consider what improvements could be made for the next time.

What Worked?	What Could Be Improved?
Relationship: Sonia trusts that coaching is helping her perform her job more effectively.	Sonia still wants to rush through the session to return to her work.
Process: Sonia has learned to listen more carefully to others.	Sonia could be more open to different ways of viewing a problem.
Results: Sonia clearly understands the steps in the process.	Sonia could practice more on the job.

How to Customize
Your Coaching

People learn in different ways depending on their personalities and studying habits. Some people can be shown how to perform a task once, and they have it. Some may have to see it repeated once or twice. Other people need to hear instructions; still others prefer learning by reading. Finding out how a particular person learns will save both you and the coachee time and frustration in the coaching process. The most effective way to discover a person's learning preference is simply to ask him. Each person knows best what method he prefers.

Selecting a coaching style

Not all people or situations are the same, so you need to master some different coaching styles to adapt to different circumstances. In some cases you need to adopt a direct approach, particularly when working with coachees who are inexperienced or whose performance requires improvement. Other situations call for supportive coaching when you act more as a facilitator or guide.

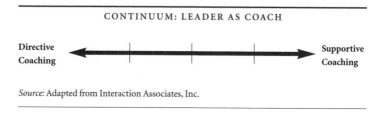

CONTINUUM: LEADER AS COACH

Directive Coaching ⟷ Supportive Coaching

Source: Adapted from Interaction Associates, Inc.

Directive versus Supportive Coaching

COACHING STYLE	USED FOR:	EXAMPLES:
Directive	Developing skills	• Instructing a new employee who needs to develop skills in your area of expertise. • Acting as a model for the coachee by showing her the most effective way to perform a task.
	Providing answers	• Explaining the company's business strategy to a new employee. • Clarifying departmental protocol for the new employee.
Supportive	Facilitating problem solving	• Helping others to find their own answers to problems.
	Building self-confidence	• Expressing confidence that an individual can find the solution. • Providing positive feedback for a job well done.
	Encouraging employees to learn on their own	• Challenging employees by assigning new responsibilities, even if it means risking mistakes.
	Serving as a resource for others	• Providing information about new situations. • Sharing experiences. • Introducing new contacts.

What Would YOU Do?

Go, Fight, Win!

BRIAN LEARNED EVERYTHING HE KNEW about coaching from Mr. Morton, his high school basketball coach. Brian learned to be tough. He learned to be kind. He learned how to get two team players who hated each other to work together. Most of all, Brian learned to keep the energy level high because that's what it takes to win. Everyone Brian had ever coached improved their performance; everyone, that is, except his two newest recruits. These kids looked good on paper. They came highly recommended, and they were competent and hard working, but they did not respond to his "go, fight, win" attitude. One of them even seemed to cringe every time Brian tried to teach her something different. Brian knew that neither one of them had ever played team sports, and he feared that they might be uncoachable. He was not one to give up, but what could he do that he hadn't tried already?

Directive coaching is used more often with new employees who need extra attention to get them going in their new jobs or with employees who need to learn a new skill.

Supportive coaching is especially important for those performers who meet current standards of performance and need to prepare to take on new or greater responsibilities. With this group, be sure to

- recognize the good work they are doing. Without making promises, indicate that opportunities for advancement are available.

- enter into a realistic and open-ended discussion of career goals

- identify the knowledge, skills, and commitment needed for different career possibilities

- ask them in what areas they see a need for growth and development to qualify for new job opportunities

- work to develop a mutually acceptable plan for acquiring the requisite skills and knowledge

- follow up on that plan at regular intervals with measurement and feedback

- invite them to use their experience and expertise to coach others

Combine the roles of evaluator and coach

Managers often feel a tension between the roles of evaluator and coach. The two roles are interrelated. As evaluator, you review the performance of your direct reports. As coach, you look for ways to help them grow and improve. This combination can be difficult for those whom you coach. Direct reports may be hesitant to bring up mistakes or shortcomings with you—for fear of admitting errors that will affect their performance evaluations. If enough of your direct reports feel this way, you won't have a clear picture of what's going on around you. This, in turn, may affect your ability to manage and meet your group's goals.

The key to managing the dual roles of evaluator and coach is creating an atmosphere of trust. Employees report that they seek help and learn best from managers who show interest in their long-term development and who provide both support and autonomy. Employees open up to managers they trust. Trust makes coaching possible, and the act of coaching itself increases trust.

Effective coaching is an upward spiral with trust at its foundation.

What You COULD Do.

Remember Brian's dilemma?

The mentor suggests:

First, Brian might clear his own mind by asking himself what's going on in this situation for him. Is he frustrated, judgmental, worried about his own competence as a coach, or just plain irritated with the two team members? To be an effective coach, he may need to consciously set these kinds of thoughts and feelings aside, so that he's not inadvertently acting on them. Then, he could have private one-on-one conversations with each player to learn about their experience levels and their hopes for being on the team. To make his intentions clear, he'll probably need to acknowledge right away that he sees they're having a tough time and that he wants to support them any way he can. Based on a solid understanding of each person's needs, he can customize an approach that has a better chance of working. They may never be stars, but then again, who knows? In the diverse world we live in, a smart coach is always ready to flex a tried-and-true style to help unleash someone's hidden potential.

Tips and Tools

Tools for
Coaching People

The Coach's Planning Form

*Use this form before a coaching session. Take the time to specify exactly
what you hope to achieve and how you intend to go about it.*

Discussion with: **Date:**

Areas Where Coaching Is Needed *(base this on observations)*:

Purpose of Coaching Session:

Desired Outcomes:

Why It's Important to Coach (*e.g., What is at stake? What are the consequences?*):

Potential Difficulties	Methods for Handling
1.	1.
2.	2.
3.	3.

Specific Actions

1.

2.

3.

Adapted with permission from AT&T.

Active Listening Self-Assessment

Are You an Active Listener?

Coaches who listen actively tend to get the most out of their coaching discussions and tend to be better coaches overall. Use this self-assessment to think about how actively you listen. Check the box next to the number in the column that best describes your listening habits.

While someone is talking, I:	Usually	Sometimes	Rarely
Plan how I'm going to respond.	❑ 1	❑ 3	❑ 5
Keep eye contact with the speaker.	❑ 5	❑ 3	❑ 1
Take notes as appropriate.	❑ 5	❑ 3	❑ 1
Notice the feeling behind the words.	❑ 5	❑ 3	❑ 1
Find myself thinking about other things while the person is talking.	❑ 1	❑ 3	❑ 5
Face the person who is talking.	❑ 5	❑ 3	❑ 1
Watch for significant body language (expressions, gestures).	❑ 5	❑ 3	❑ 1
Interrupt the speaker to make a point.	❑ 1	❑ 3	❑ 5
Am distracted by other demands on my time.	❑ 1	❑ 3	❑ 5
Listen to the message without immediately judging or evaluating it.	❑ 5	❑ 3	❑ 1
Ask questions to get more information and encourage the speaker to continue.	❑ 5	❑ 3	❑ 1
Repeat in my own words what I've just heard to ensure understanding.	❑ 5	❑ 3	❑ 1
Totals for each column:	_____ +	_____ +	_____
Grand Total =	_____		

Scoring:

44 – 60 = You are an active listener.

28 – 43 = You are a good listener with room for improvement.

12 – 27 = You need to focus on improving your listening skills.

Source: AT&T School of Business. *The Supervisor: Coaching for Success.* AT&T School of Business, 1995.

A Coach's Self-Evaluation Checklist

The questions below relate to the skills and qualities needed to be an effective coach.
Use this tool to evaluate your own effectiveness as a coach.

Question	Yes	No
1. Do you show interest in career development, not just short-term performance?		
2. Do you provide both support and autonomy?		
3. Do you set high yet attainable goals?		
4. Do you serve as a role model?		
5. Do you communicate business strategies and expected behaviors as a basis for establishing objectives?		
6. Do you work with the individual you are coaching to generate alternative approaches or solutions that you can consider together?		
7. Before giving feedback, do you observe carefully, and without bias, the individual you are coaching?		
8. Do you separate observations from judgments or assumptions?		
9. Do you test your theories about a person's behavior before acting on them?		
10. Are you careful to avoid using your own performance as a yardstick to measure others?		
11. Do you focus your attention and avoid distractions when someone is talking to you?		
12. Do you paraphrase or use some other method to clarify what is being said in a discussion?		
13. Do you use relaxed body language and verbal cues to encourage a speaker during conversations?		

Question	Yes	No
14. Do you use open-ended questions to promote sharing of ideas and information?		
15. Do you give specific feedback?		
16. Do you give timely feedback?		
17. Do you give feedback that focuses on behavior and its consequences (rather than on vague judgments)?		
18. Do you give positive as well as negative feedback?		
19. Do you try to reach agreement on desired goals and outcomes rather than simply dictate them?		
20. Do you try to prepare for coaching discussions in advance?		
21. Do you always follow up on a coaching discussion to make sure progress is proceeding as planned?		
TOTALS		

When you have these characteristics and use these strategies, people trust you and turn to you for both professional and personal support. If you answered "yes" to most of these questions, you are probably an effective coach. If you answered "no" to some or many of these questions, you may want to consider how you can further develop your coaching skills.

Action-Planning Worksheet

Use this worksheet to establish an action plan that is agreeable to both you and the person you are coaching. It is critical to include specific measures of success and a target review date for any actions to be completed. Examples are included.

Action to Be Taken	Measure(s) of Success	Review

Coaching Session Evaluation

Use this tool after the coaching session to evaluate its effectiveness and to consider what improvements could be made for the next time.

What Worked?	What Could Be Improved?
Relationship:	
Process:	
Results:	

Test Yourself

Test Yourself offers ten multiple choice questions to help you identify your baseline knowledge of professional coaching.

Answers to the questions are given at the end of the test.

1. Which of the following statements is a FALSE description of what coaching is?

   a. Coaching is guiding someone toward his or her goals.

   b. Coaching is a means for learning and developing.

   c. Coaching is an opportunity to correct someone's behaviors or actions.

2. Because coaching is based on mutual agreement, it is not always an appropriate strategy. Which of the following situations requires direct intervention, rather than coaching?

   a. While giving a report at a meeting, one of your direct reports seems nervous about delivering bad news.

   b. A customer you have worked with previously tells you that your direct report couldn't answer some product questions.

   c. You overhear a direct report promising a customer something that is not available.

3. When should coaching take place?

    a. As the need arises.

    b. Formally yearly; informally quarterly.

    c. At least once a quarter.

4. When is it more appropriate to use an open-ended question than a close-ended question?

    a. When you are focusing on the response or confirming what has been said.

    b. When you are exploring alternatives or uncovering attitudes or needs.

5. While you are conducting a coaching session, which of the following guidelines is FALSE?

    a. Generate alternatives—focus the coaching on at least three coaching topic alternatives.

    b. Focus on behavior—not character, attitude, or personality.

    c. Be specific. Avoid generalization.

6. What might happen if you over-rely on using questions or inquiry as a coaching strategy?

    a. The coachee may begin to withhold important information and perspectives.

    b. You may not have an opportunity to express your own ideas adequately.

    c. You may limit elaboration of different options.

7. During the coaching process, when as coach should you provide feedback?

    a. Only after all views have been discussed.

    b. At the end of each coaching session.

    c. Early and often.

8. Which coaching style might be most appropriate for explaining a business strategy to a new employee?

    a. supportive

    b. authoritative

    c. direct

9. For what group of individuals is supportive coaching especially important?

    a. Individuals who do not meet current standards of performance and who are anxious about their performance.

    b. Individuals who meet current performance standards and who need to prepare to take on new or greater responsibilities.

    c. Individuals who need instruction about how to complete an assignment they have not attempted before.

10. What is the most important aspect of effective coaching?

    a. Gaining trust.

    b. Listening actively.

    c. Choosing the most appropriate coaching style.

Answers to test questions

1, c. Coaching is NOT an opportunity to correct someone's behavior or actions. It IS a two-way partnership, a means for both partners to learn and develop.

2, c. Direct intervention is appropriate when someone clearly violates company policy or organizational values.

3, a. Unlike goal-setting or performance reviews, which are scheduled quarterly or yearly, effective coaching is ongoing. Sometimes coaching focuses on specific situations. Often, however, coaching is informal and happens on the go as you interact with direct reports or peers—in person, by phone, or even through e-mail.

4, b. Open-ended questions invite participation and idea-sharing whereas close-ended questions lead to "yes" or "no" answers. When you want to find out more about another person's motivations and feelings, use open-ended questions. The responses will give more information that will help you to understand their perspectives.

5, a. For effective coaching, keep the coaching limited to one or two topics.

6, a. A balance between inquiry and advocacy is generally the most effective coaching strategy. A balanced approach allows coaches to offer their ideas and advice in such a way that the coachees can hear them, respond to them, and consider their value.

7, c. Frequent feedback that is delivered during a discussion is more effective than infrequent feedback given at the end of a session.

8, c. The direct approach is most helpful when working with individuals who are inexperienced.

9, b. Individuals who need to prepare for new or greater responsibilities most need supportive coaching. Be sure to acknowledge their good work.

10, a. Trust between coach and coachee is essential for a successful coaching relationship.

To Learn More

Notes and Articles

Richard Bierck. "How to Listen: Listening Is an Integral Part of Good Business Communication." *Harvard Management Communication Letter.* January 2001.

> Listening effectively takes planning, discipline, and attention. Even though some people seem to be naturally better listeners than others, everyone can learn to listen more carefully.

Martha Craumer. "How to Coach Your Employees: Focus on Their Strengths, Not Their Weakensses." *Harvard Management Communication Letter.* December 2001.

> The most successful managerial coaching focuses on employees' strengths and building on them. Showing respect and trust is the key to influencing your employees to respond to coaching and achieve results.

James Waldroop and Timothy Butler. "The Executive as Coach." *Harvard Business Review* OnPoint Enhanced Edition. Boston: Harvard Business School Publishing, 2000.

> How do you deal with the talented manager whose perfectionism paralyzes his direct reports or the high-performing expert

who disdains teamwork? What about the sensitive manager who avoids confrontation of any kind? Get rid of them? The authors suggest that you coach them; helping to change the behaviors that threaten to derail a valued manager is often the best way to help that manager succeed. Executives increasingly recognize that people management skills are the key to both their personal success and the success of their businesses. And being an effective coach is a crucial part of successful people management.

Books

Chip R. Bell. *Managers as Mentors: Building Partnerships for Learning.* San Francisco: Berrett-Koehler, 1998.

This hands-on guide takes the mystery out of effective mentoring, teaching leaders to be the kind of confident coaches integral to learning organizations.

Jerry W. Gilley and Nathaniel W. Boughton. *Stop Managing, Start Coaching! How Performance Coaching Can Enhance Commitment and Improve Productivity.* Chicago: Irwin Professional Publishing, 1996.

This book on performance coaching describes how managers can balance the roles of trainer, mentor, and career coach to improve workplace productivity.

Harvard Business School Publishing. *Coaching Collection. Harvard Business Review* Collection. Boston: Harvard Business School Publishing, 1997.

This collection presents ideas, practices, and tools to improve the leadership and decision-making skills of employees.

Harvard Business School Publishing. *Making Your Best Performers Better. Harvard Business Review* OnPoint Collection. Boston: Harvard Business School Publishing, 2001.

You've got a perplexing problem: highly promising performers who are so close to being great—if they could just get over a critical hurdle. One inexplicably won't support a key change initiative. Another has a career-threatening personality flaw. Yet another lacks the passion for his job that you would expect. Tempted to get rid of all these folks? Before you do, consider the situation in a different light: Really talented employees are notoriously hard to find and keep. And letting their potential waste away while they're with you is costly. Helping these employees surmount barriers to their success can pay big dividends for them and for your company as a whole.

Richard R. Kilburg. *Executive Coaching: Developing Managerial Wisdom in a World of Chaos.* Washington, D.C.: APA, 2000.

Kilburg provides a holistic view of coaching, showing how systems can be integrated into real-world coaching problems. In the complex and unpredictable world of business, Kilburg offers a practical and understandable guide for coaches to learn more about how to have a meaningful impact on behavior. Kilburg uses case studies, tables, and models for easy comprehension of a complex topic.

Florence M. Stone. *Coaching, Counseling, and Mentoring: How to Choose and Use the Right Technique to Boost Employee Performance.* New York: AMACOM, 1999.

The book clearly defines and describes each role, shows readers how to adapt skills to specific situations, demonstrates through case examples how the skill is used in practice, and gives advice on how to avoid common traps and problems. Each section also includes a chapter on how to use the skills with teams as well as individuals.

eLearning Products

Harvard Business School Publishing. *Coaching for Results.* Boston: Harvard Business School Publishing, 2000. Online program.

Understand and practice how to effectively coach others by mastering the five core skills necessary for successful coaching:

- observing
- questioning
- listening
- feedback
- agreement

Through interactive role-play, expert guidance, and activities for immediate application at work, this program helps you coach successfully by teaching you how to prepare, discuss, and follow-up in any situation.

Harvard Business School Publishing. *Influencing and Motivating Others.* Boston: Harvard Business School Publishing, 2001. Online program.

Have you ever noticed how some people seem to have a natural ability to stir others to action? *Influencing and Motivating Others* provides actionable lessons on getting better results from direct reports (influencing performance), greater cooperation from your peers (lateral leadership), and stronger support from your own boss and senior management (persuasion). Managers will learn the secrets of "lateral leadership" (leading peers), negotiation and persuasion skills, and how to distinguish between effective and ineffective motivation methods. Through interactive cases, expert guidance, and activities for immediate application at work, this program helps managers to assess their ability to effectively persuade others, measure motivation skills, and enhance employee performance.

Sources for Coaching People

We would like to acknowledge the sources that aided in developing this topic.

At&T School of Business. *The Supervisor: Coaching for Success.* AT&T School of Business, 1995.

Richard Bierck, financial writer

Martha Craumer, business writer

Stan Hustad, PTM Group

Patty McManus, consultant, Interaction Associates

Notes

Notes

Notes

Notes

Notes

Notes

Notes

Notes

Notes

Notes

Notes

Notes

Notes

How to Order

Harvard Business School Press publications are available world-wide from your local bookseller or online retailer.

You can also call:
1-800-668-6780

Our product consultants are available to help you 8:00 a.m.–6:00 p.m., Monday–Friday, Eastern time. Outside the U.S. and Canada, call: 617-783-7450.

Please call about special discounts for quantities greater than ten.

You can order online at:
www.HBSPress.org